# AN AUNT'S GUIDEBOOK TO...

## BUILDING MEMORIES & HAVING FUN!

## LEAH HOLLERAN

*I dedicate this book to my nieces and nephews, whose presence illuminates my existence. The time I share with them is invaluable, brimming with laughter and endless oy. They are my heart's delight, the inspiration behind these pages, and the reason our memories together are so deeply cherished.*

# CONTENTS

# INTRODUCTION

Being an aunt is an experience like no other. It's a role filled with laughter, love, and the unique opportunity to be a part of a child's life in a profound and playful way. This book is born from incredible relationships and the countless memories I've cherished with my nieces and nephews. It's for anyone who, like me, has found joy and purpose in the playful hours spent with the younger members of our families. Whether you're an aunt, an uncle, or a parent, this guide is a treasure trove of ideas to help you make the most of your time with the children in your life.

I've always harbored a deep desire to have children, but life, as it often does, had other plans. This twist of fate, however, led me to discover the next best thing: being an aunt. It's a role that has brought me immeasurable joy and fulfillment. Watching my sister excel in her journey as a mother has been nothing short of inspiring. Her innate ability to nurture and create a loving environment has taught me much about the role model I want to be. Through her example and my own experiences, I've gathered the insights and activities shared in this book.

The essence of this guide is to provide you with a collection of activities that foster fun, creativity, and connection. From outdoor adventures that spark curiosity and excitement to indoor games that conjure imagination and laughter, there's something here for every occasion. But it's not just about the activities themselves; it's about the moments they create, the bonds they strengthen, and the memories they leave behind. These experiences are precious, not only for the children but for us as adults. They remind us of the joy of play, the beauty of simplicity, and the importance of being present.

It's important to note that while many of the ideas in this book are geared toward younger children, there are plenty of suggestions older kids will enjoy, too. After all, fun has no age limit. This guide will inspire you to explore new ways to engage with children through planned activities or spontaneous play. Each chapter offers various options, ensuring you have a go-to resource for creating memorable experiences regardless of the weather, setting, or mood.

As we embark on this journey together, I invite you to keep an open heart and mind. The true magic of spending time with children is in the activities you choose and the love and laughter you share. This book is more than just a collection of ideas; it's a celebration of the joy, challenges, and unexpected moments of being an integral part of a child's life.

As we transition into the first chapter, we'll dive into a world of outdoor fun. I'll share some of my favorite activities that have entertained my nieces and nephews and allowed us to explore, learn, and grow together under the open sky. Get ready to step outside, embrace the adventure, and create lasting memories you'll treasure forever.

Let's turn the page and discover the endless possibilities that await us. Together, we'll learn how to make every moment count, creating a tapestry of memories that will enrich our lives and those of the children we adore. Welcome to "An Aunt's Guidebook To... Making Memories & Having Fun!"

# FUN OUTSIDE

S tepping outside opens a world of fun, adventure, and learning possibilities. This chapter is dedicated to exploring outdoor activities that are both a blast for kids and fantastic opportunities for you to build beautiful memories together. Each activity encourages creativity, physical activity, and a deeper connection with the natural world. Let's dive into the joyful world of outdoor play, where every day promises a new adventure.

## GARDENING

Gardening is a tactile and rewarding way to introduce kids to the wonders of the natural world and the satisfaction that comes from nurturing life. This activity combines learning about nature with lessons in responsibility and patience as children witness a plant's journey from seed to bloom or harvest. Starting with simple projects, such as planting flowers known for their resilience or vegetables that promise quick and visible rewards, can spark an interest that grows as steadily as plants.

The very act of gardening—digging in the soil, carefully placing seeds or seedlings, and providing water and care—offers a deeply satisfying experience for children. There's a certain magic in getting their hands dirty, a sensory play that's both educational and fun. It connects them directly with the life cycle, teaching them about the conditions plants need to grow and the factors that can influence their health.

Involving kids in the ongoing care of the plants is crucial to enhancing the gardening experience. Dead-heading, the process of removing dead or spent flowers, is an excellent way for children to contribute to the garden's well-being. This activity keeps the garden looking its best and encourages plants to produce more flowers, extending the blooming season and offering more opportunities for engagement and learning.

Another enriching aspect of gardening is teaching kids how to collect and spread seeds from mature plants. Children can learn that with care and attention, a single plant can produce seeds that lead to the growth of many new plants, fostering a cycle of growth and renewal they can witness and influence from start to finish.

Gardening with kids is more than just a pastime; it's an educational journey encompassing lessons in biology, ecology, and environmental stewardship. It encourages curiosity, fosters a sense of achievement, and cultivates an appreciation for the natural world. By starting small and supporting their interests and efforts, you can help nurture a garden and a lifelong love for growing and caring for living things

## BUG HOUSES / FAERIE HOUSES

Building bug houses or faerie houses taps into children's boundless imagination. It invites them to create enchanting shelters using the simplicity and beauty of natural materials. This activity serves as a canvas for creativity and offers valuable lessons on the importance of natural habitats, fostering an early appreciation for the environment and its many inhabitants.

Gather natural materials from your surroundings to embark on this magical construction project. Twigs, leaves, bark, stones, and fallen flowers are perfect for crafting these tiny abodes. Encourage children to think about the structure and design of their houses, considering what materials would work best for walls, roofs, and decorative elements. This process stimulates critical thinking and problem-solving skills as they figure out how to assemble their materials into a stable structure.

Creating bug houses allows children to explore the concept of shelters and habitats, understanding how different creatures seek refuge and safety. Discussing the types of bugs that might inhabit these houses can extend the learning opportunity, introducing basic biology and ecology in a hands-on, engaging way.

On the other hand, Faerie houses open a door to a world of fantasy and storytelling. Encouraging children to imagine the faeries that might visit or reside in their crafted houses can spark creative storytelling, drawing connections between the natural world and the fantastical stories they create. This imaginative play enriches their cognitive and creative development, blending art, nature, and narrative into a captivating activity.

This endeavor is about the end product and the process —exploring nature, handling and appreciating its offerings, and learning to create something meaningful from them. It's a peaceful, contemplative activity that can be as much about quiet reflection and connection with the natural world as it is about creative expression.

In constructing bug houses or faerie houses, children not only leave with a tangible reminder of their creativity and connection to nature but also gain an understanding of the symbiotic relationships that sustain the natural world. This project encourages them to see themselves as part of a larger ecosystem, fostering a sense of stewardship and wonder for the environment that will grow as they do.

## PAINTING ROCKS

Collecting and painting rocks can be a fun and creative outdoor activity. Kids can turn their painted rocks into garden markers, gifts, or hidden treasures for others to find. This activity allows for artistic expression and can be a calming, meditative practice.

## MAGIC STATUE

Magic Statue is a playful and engaging game combining elements of freeze tag and creative posing. It is perfect for energizing any outdoor gathering. In this game, one person is designated as "it" and has the power to freeze players, turning them into "statues." The twist? These statues are not merely frozen in place; they can change locations and poses, adding elements of strategy and surprise.

The game begins with "it" closing their eyes or turning their back, allowing the statues to scatter and strike a pose. The statues must remain perfectly still, embodying the essence of a statue. The challenge comes when "it" turns to observe the statues; the statues must remain as motionless as possible, even as "it" walks among them, inspecting their poses.

The moment "it" turns its back again, the statues come to life, silently moving to a new location to assume a new pose. The goal for the statues is to change positions without being caught by "it" in the act of moving. If "it" catches a statue moving, that round ends, and roles are reassigned for the next round of play.

Magic Statue tests physical agility and stealth and is a wonderful outlet for creativity. Players can create unique and imaginative poses, transforming the game into a dynamic and hilarious spectacle. The game encourages laughter, movement, and the joy of play, making it a memorable addition to any outdoor activity lineup.

Magic Statue is a delightful way to engage with children and encourage them to exercise their bodies and imaginations. Gather your group, designate your "it," and let the statues come to life in this enchanting game of movement and creativity.

## CHASE

Chase is a timeless game that needs no introduction. It is all about running and laughter, whether a simple tag game or a more structured game like cops and robbers. It's a fantastic way to get kids moving and using up energy.

## DUCK, DUCK, GOOSE

This classic game is perfect for groups and fosters community and fun. Sitting in a circle, one person walks around tapping heads and saying "duck" until they choose someone to be the "goose," who must chase them around the circle to take their spot.

## COMPETITIONS

Competitions are a fantastic way to inject excitement and a spirit of challenge into outdoor play. Simple yet immensely enjoyable, they offer many benefits, from promoting physical activity to teaching valuable lessons about healthy competition and striving for personal improvement. Organizing these contests should always focus on fun, inclusivity, and personal growth rather than solely on winning or losing.

Races are a classic starting point. They can be as straightforward as sprinting from one end of the yard to the other or as creative as a three-legged or sack race. The key is to vary the types to keep engagement high and to cater to different skill levels and interests.

Jumping contests offer another avenue for energetic competition. Whether the challenge is to see who can jump the farthest from a standing position or complete the most jumps in a minute, the challenges can be adapted to suit the space available and the participants' age groups.

Skipping challenges add a rhythmic and coordination-based element to the competition roster. They can range from counting the number of skips in a set time to trickier competitions for those more adept. Skipping is fun and an excellent cardiovascular exercise that improves coordination and stamina.

When organizing these competitions, it's essential to frame them within the context of healthy competition. Emphasize the joy of participation, the thrill of setting and achieving personal goals, and the importance of sportsmanship. Celebrate every effort, not just the first to finish or the highest jumper, and encourage children to reflect on their personal bests and how they might improve in a supportive, non-pressurized environment. Participating in these simple contests teaches children that striving for personal improvement and supporting their peers are rewarding experiences that transcend the playground.

## TREASURE MAP MAKING & HUNTING

Treasure map-making and hunting are exhilarating activities that bring the thrill of adventure and exploration right to your backyard or local park. This activity ignites the imagination and engages children in a hands-on experience of problem-solving and discovery. The beauty of treasure hunting lies in its flexibility; it can be tailored to fit any age group, location, and group size, making it a versatile addition to your outdoor activity repertoire.

To begin, you'll need to create a treasure map, which can be a fun and creative process. Start with a piece of paper and draw a map of your outdoor area. You can add landmarks, X marks the spot for the treasure, and even weave in obstacles or challenges to reach the treasure. The map can be as straightforward or as cryptic as you like, depending on the age and abilities of the treasure hunters.

Next, decide on the treasure. It could be anything from a box of treats to a collection of small toys or trinkets. Hide the treasure in the designated spot and ensure your map accurately leads to its location. For an added layer of intrigue, you can include clues or riddles at various points that must be solved to proceed to the next map stage.

The hunt begins once the map is ready and the treasure is hidden. Hand the map to the children and watch them embark on their quest. As they navigate the clues and landmarks, they'll hone their problem-solving skills and learn the value of teamwork if they work in a group. This activity is not just about finding the treasure; it's about the journey, overcoming challenges, and the joy of discovery.

Treasure map making and hunting offer a unique blend of physical activity, creative expression, and cognitive challenge, making it an enriching experience for children. It's an opportunity for them to immerse themselves in a world of adventure, where they're the heroes of their own story, navigating the wilds of the great outdoors in search of hidden treasure. So, gather your materials, let your creativity flow in designing a captivating treasure map, and prepare for an unforgettable adventure children will talk about long after the treasure has been found.

## HIDE & SEEK (INSIDE OR OUTSIDE)

Hide-and-seek is a versatile game that can be played in nearly any outdoor space. It encourages strategic thinking and can be thrilling in stealth and surprise. Plus, it can easily be adapted for all ages.

## MAKE AND DO AN OBSTACLE COURSE

Creating an obstacle course presents an exciting challenge, physically and mentally engaging children. It is a dynamic way to promote fitness, agility, and creative thinking. The beauty of setting up an obstacle course lies in its versatility and adaptability. You can use everyday items found in your yard, home, or local park to construct a series of challenges that require jumping, crawling, and balancing and are as unique as they are fun.

To begin, survey the area for potential obstacles and items that can be safely used to create your course. The goal is to include a variety of tasks that test different skills: jumping over a rope or a soft object, crawling under a string stretched between two points, weaving through a series of cones or makeshift markers, and balancing along a designated path or a narrow beam.

Designing and setting up the course is an exercise in creative problem-solving, not just for you but for the kids involved. Encourage them to contribute ideas for obstacles, turning the setup into a collaborative project. This inclusion boosts their investment in the activity and stimulates their imagination and planning skills.

As children navigate the course, they move their bodies and learn to assess challenges, adapt their strategies, and overcome physical and mental barriers. It can be an empowering experience, fostering a sense of achievement and confidence with each completed run.

Moreover, the obstacle course can be easily modified to suit different ages and abilities, ensuring everyone can participate and enjoy the challenge. As children grow and develop, the course can be updated to reflect their changing skills and interests, providing a continually evolving playground that keeps them active and engaged.

## FLY A KITE

Flying a kite is akin to performing a delicate dance with the wind, which invites both the young and the young at heart to engage in a playful tussle with the breeze. It's about more than just watching a colorful tail flutter against the backdrop of a clear sky; it's an experience that connects us with the elements, allowing us to touch the sky and revel in the beauty of a perfect day. This simple pleasure, accessible to all ages, embodies the thrill of guiding a soaring kite as it climbs higher, responding to the ebb and flow of the wind.

Kite flying is about control and letting go, feeling the kite's pull, and witnessing it dance gracefully above. It teaches patience, attentiveness, and the joy of success when the kite catches the wind just right. Whether alone, with friends, or as a family, flying a kite turns an ordinary day outdoors into an extraordinary adventure. It fills the sky with color and life, leaving us with a sense of accomplishment and awe of the world above and around us.

## PLAY FOLLOW THE LEADER

Follow the Leader is a game of mimicry and imagination, a journey led by one, with each step and action mirrored by the rest. The designated leader guides the group through a series of movements, adventures, and challenges, from hopping on one foot to navigating obstacles in the outdoor setting. It's a test of creativity for the leader and a challenge of attentiveness for the followers, making it a dynamic and engaging activity for children of all ages. This game fosters physical coordination and agility and encourages participants to think creatively as they invent new actions for the group. Whether winding through a garden, tiptoeing across a line, or gesturing wildly under the open sky, Follow the Leader celebrates leadership, trust, and the simple joy of moving together in harmony.

## JUMP ROPE

Jump Rope is an exhilarating activity that seamlessly blends rhythm and coordination, inviting kids to leap over the swinging rope in sync with its beat. This simple yet captivating game can be enjoyed individually, with the challenge of mastering intricate steps and jumps or fostering teamwork and synchronization in double Dutch variations as a group. It tests timing and agility, encouraging players to maintain a steady pace while navigating the rope's arc. Beyond the physical benefits of improved coordination and cardiovascular health, jump rope inspires a sense of achievement as children set and reach new goals, whether mastering a new trick or achieving a personal best in consecutive jumps. This activity, rooted in play, offers a fun and engaging way for children to explore the limits of their bodies, develop a sense of rhythm, and enjoy the exhilarating feeling of soaring through the air with each jump.

## PLAY SPORTS

Playing sports introduces children to teamwork, skill development, and the exhilaration of active participation. Whether team sports like soccer and basketball or individual pursuits like swimming, each activity offers unique lessons. Team sports emphasize cooperation and communication, teaching players to work towards common goals and gracefully handle wins and losses. Individual sports focus on personal goal-setting, self-discipline, and the satisfaction of personal achievement, encouraging children to push their limits.

Beyond the physical benefits, sports enhance strategic thinking and patience, combining physical action with mental discipline. Also, the camaraderie, resilience, and sportsmanship learned through play make playing sports a valuable experience. These activities offer more than just exercise; they provide life lessons in a context of fun and competition, shaping skills and attitudes that extend far beyond the playing field.

As we conclude this chapter, remember that the ultimate goal of these activities is not just to keep kids entertained but to foster a deep and lasting connection with them through shared experiences. Each activity is a building block in the foundation of their childhood memories, providing endless opportunities for learning, exploration, and fun. So, lace up your shoes, slather on the sunscreen, and create a world of outdoor adventures that everyone will cherish for years to come.

2

# MEMORIES MADE INSIDE

Rainy days and cozy afternoons indoors offer the perfect backdrop for creating unforgettable memories with the young ones in your life. Inside the comfort of your home, a world of imagination and fun awaits, ready to transform any ordinary day into an extraordinary adventure. This chapter is dedicated to exploring a variety of indoor activities that promise not only to entertain but also to forge lasting bonds and cherished memories between you and the children you care for. From the simplest joys of crafting and story-telling to the exuberant energy of dance parties and cooking adventures, there's something here for every interest and occasion.

## BLANKET FORTS

Constructing a blanket fort is a classic childhood delight that never fails to excite. Using blankets, pillows, and furniture, you can create a magical kingdom or a cozy hideout in your living room. This activity encourages creativity and problem-solving as kids figure out how to structure their fort, and it provides a unique space for them to play, imagine, and even relax with books or toys.

## SQUIGGLE DRAWINGS & STORY

Squiggle drawings and stories breathe life into the art of storytelling, transforming a mere doodle into an entire world of imagination. The adventure begins with a simple squiggle on a piece of paper—an aimless line or curve with endless possibilities. This initial squiggle is handed to the child, who is invited to let their imagination soar as they turn this random line into a detailed drawing. It might become a curious creature, a fantastical vehicle, a bizarre plant, or anything their heart desires.

The real magic begins once the transformation from squiggle to drawing is complete. Together, we delve into storytelling by giving this new creation a name, a story, a home, and even a diet. Discuss its adventures, its friends, its fears, and its dreams. What does it do during the day? What makes it laugh? Where does it find comfort? This process does more than just flesh out a story; it opens a doorway to understanding the child's thoughts, feelings, and imaginative methods.

The activity of squiggle drawings and stories is a powerful tool for fostering creativity and interpretive thinking. It encourages children to see beyond the obvious, to imbue life and narrative into something as simple as a squiggle. Moreover, shared storytelling strengthens the bond between you and the child. By actively listening to their ideas and contributing your own, you create a collaborative space where creativity is valued and imagination is boundless.

## DANCE PARTY / FREEZE DANCE

An indoor dance party or a game of freeze dance is a fantastic way to get moving and laughing. Play your favorite tunes and let loose with your best dance moves. For the freeze dance, pause the music at random intervals, and everyone must freeze in their current pose until the music starts again. This activity is excellent for physical exercise and creating a joyful and carefree atmosphere.

## CRAFTY COLLAGE

A crafty collage is a vibrant canvas for artistic expression, inviting children to explore textures, colors, and shapes tangibly and joyfully. This activity begins with the gathering of materials, which can include a wide array of items: magazines, old photos, colored paper, glue, feathers, yarn, rhinestones, scraps of fabric, glitter, stickers, paint, and colored crayons. The diversity of materials encourages exploration and experimentation, allowing children to mix and match elements as their creativity dictates.

Whether you guide them towards creating a themed collage—perhaps centered around a holiday, a favorite animal, or a dream destination—or simply let their imagination guide their choices for a freestyle creation, the process is equally rewarding. Encouraging children to think about composition, color balance, and thematic relevance can enrich their understanding of visual artistry while allowing ample room for personal expression.

As they select and arrange their materials, children make decisions and solve problems, learning to envision the final piece and how each component contributes to the overall effect. This hands-on activity not only hones their artistic skills but also provides a tactile, engaging experience that can be therapeutic and immensely satisfying.

The finished crafty collage can serve as a cherished keepsake, a snapshot of creativity and imagination that captures the moment's essence. It can be proudly displayed, shared with family and friends, or even given as a gift, adding a personal touch that celebrates the child's artistic journey.

Beyond the sheer fun and artistic exploration, creating a crafty collage with children is an opportunity to bond, share insights and laughs over the selection of pictures and materials, and marvel at each child's unique vision. It reminds us that art isn't just about the end product but the joy and discovery in the process, fostering a love for creative expression that can last a lifetime.

## BAKING & COOKING

Inviting kids into the kitchen for baking and cooking sessions is a flavorful journey that blends the art of culinary creation with the warmth of making memories together. Choosing simple, engaging recipes ensures that children can participate fully in the process, from measuring and mixing to the final touches that make each dish unique. Activities like decorating cookies, assembling personal pizzas, or creating fruit kebabs allow for hands-on participation and offer a canvas for creativity and individual expression.

This shared kitchen adventure is about more than just preparing food; it's an opportunity to teach valuable life skills such as following instructions, measuring ingredients, and understanding the importance of timing and safety in cooking. As children watch ingredients transform into something delicious, they experience the magic of creation and the satisfaction of contributing to a meal.

Moreover, cooking and baking together fosters a sense of accomplishment and togetherness. There's a special joy in sharing the results of your joint effort, whether sitting down to eat a meal you've made together or presenting friends and family with a batch of homemade treats. These moments of shared pride and enjoyment are the ingredients for lasting memories.

## TOY HUNTING (MORPHS FOR EACH HOLIDAY)

Hosting a themed toy hunt in your home offers an exhilarating experience for children, inviting them to search for hidden objects like balls and stuffed animals. This activity turns into a captivating adventure that goes beyond mere fun, enhancing their connection with seasonal celebrations and traditions. For example, concealing tiny hearts throughout your home for Valentine's Day, scattering shamrocks for St. Patrick's Day, or tucking away small pumpkins during the Halloween and Thanksgiving periods enriches the hunt with a festive spirit. This customized approach not only heightens their sense of wonder and expectancy but also acts as an engaging way to teach them about the significance of various holidays and seasons. By varying the themes according to the calendar, the toy hunt remains a fresh and eagerly anticipated event, creating a delightful way to mark and celebrate the changing times of the year.

## JOKE & RIDDLE MARATHONS

A joke and riddle marathon can keep the laughter going for hours. Take turns sharing your favorite jokes and riddles, or look up new ones to stump each other. This activity is great for light-hearted fun and sharing new jokes with friends.

## READING BOOKS TO ONE ANOTHER

Sharing stories through reading books to one another is a cherished activity that transcends time, offering a quiet yet deeply connective experience between adults and children. This storytelling tradition bridges the vast worlds contained within literature and nurtures a profound bond through the shared journey of narrative exploration. Reading aloud to kids opens the door to fantastical lands, intriguing characters, and complex moral tales, sparking their imagination and curiosity. This act of shared reading is more than just an educational tool; it is a means of traveling together through the realms of fantasy and reality, exploring diverse cultures, histories, and perspectives without ever leaving the room. The rhythmic cadence of a well-told story can soothe, excite, and inspire, making it an invaluable part of a child's developmental journey.

Encouraging children to take turns reading to you is equally important, as it fosters a sense of confidence and pride in their growing abilities. This role reversal allows children to practice their reading skills in a supportive environment, enhancing their language development, phonetic skills, and comprehension. It also allows them to share stories that resonate with them, providing insight into their interests and thoughts. By actively listening and engaging with the stories they choose to read aloud, adults can encourage a deeper engagement with the text, asking questions and discussing themes that further enrich the reading experience. This reciprocal exchange bolsters their reading proficiency and reinforces the value of listening, empathy, and shared learning. Through the simple act of reading together, children learn that books are treasures filled with knowledge, adventure, and emotional resonance, fostering a lifelong love of reading and learning.

## YOUTUBE MOVEMENT CHALLENGES

Leveraging online resources such as YouTube for indoor movement challenges offers children a unique opportunity to stay active and engaged, regardless of outdoor conditions. This digital platform hosts a diverse array of child-friendly activities, including yoga sessions designed to introduce children to the benefits of mindfulness and flexibility, dance tutorials that get their bodies moving to the rhythm, and imaginative games like "The Floor is Lava," which encourages quick thinking and physical agility. Additionally, obstacle challenge videos can inspire kids to create courses at home, using everyday items to foster creativity and physical fitness.

Such challenges promote physical health and help constructively expend energy. They also make these activities fun and easily accessible from the comfort of home. Children can enjoy various physical activities that cater to their interests and energy levels by participating in the online-guided exercises. It's a way to make exercise feel less like a chore and more like an exciting adventure, all while teaching valuable lessons about persistence, fitness, and the joy of movement. These YouTube challenges provide a safe and engaging platform for children to explore new types of movement, encouraging a lifelong engagement with physical activity through fun and innovation.

## PAPER AIRPLANE MAKING & FLIGHT COMPETITIONS

Crafting paper airplanes merges the simplicity of paper with the complexity of aerodynamics, offering a hands-on learning experience that's both fun and educational. This activity invites children to delve into the world of physics and creativity by designing and folding airplanes from sheets of paper. The process encourages experimentation with different folds, shapes, and weights to discover which designs yield the best flight paths or perform the most impressive aerial tricks.

Once the airplanes are ready, the excitement escalates with the initiation of flight competitions. These contests can range from seeing whose airplane flies the farthest to determining which can execute the most intricate maneuvers. This friendly competition not only adds an element of excitement but also teaches valuable lessons about trial and error, problem-solving, and the principles of flight. Children learn to adjust their designs based on the outcomes they observe, fostering a deeper understanding of how changes in design can affect performance.

Such competitions can be a fun way to engage the entire family or a group of friends, turning the activity into a shared event that everyone looks forward to. By incorporating elements of physics, engineering, and art into a single activity, paper airplane-making, and flight competitions stimulate curiosity and creativity while providing a playful platform for exploring the wonders of flight.

## BOARD GAMES

Board games are a great way to engage in strategic thinking, patience, and turn-taking. From classic games that challenge the mind to newer games designed for laughs and teamwork, there's a board game for every age and interest.

Indoor days need not be dull when you have many activities at your fingertips, ready to turn any day spent indoors into a treasure trove of happy memories. These activities are not just ways to pass the time; they are stepping stones to learning, creativity, and building closer bonds. Whether you're making forts, baking cookies, or being lost in a world of books and stories, each moment spent engaged in these activities is a precious memory in the making.

## 3

## QUIET TIME

E ven the most energetic children need moments to wind down and rest, though convincing them to embrace these quiet periods can often be challenging. Quiet time is essential for physical rest and mental and emotional balance, allowing children to process their experiences and let their imaginations roam freely. This chapter delves into activities that make quiet time engaging and restorative, ensuring that children find relaxation enjoyable rather than a chore. We can turn these moments into opportunities for creativity, storytelling, and reflection through gentle, restful activities.

## DRAWING ON BELLIES OR BACKS (WITH FINGERTIP)

A simple yet profoundly soothing activity is to draw on each other's backs or bellies with gentle fingertip movements. This game can be a calming tactile experience and a fun guessing game. One person uses a finger to draw a simple shape, letter, number, or even a rudimentary picture on the other's back or belly. The other person then guesses what was drawn. This activity promotes relaxation through gentle touch and engages children's imaginations and cognitive skills in trying to visualize and identify the shapes being drawn. It's a wonderfully intimate way to connect and share a quiet moment, offering comfort.

## TELLING STORIES

Storytelling is a timeless, quiet activity that stirs the imagination and soothes the soul. During quiet time, encourage children to listen to a story you tell or create their own stories to share. The stories can be about anything – a grand adventure, a mystery to solve, or even a day in the life of their favorite toy. Storytelling is a restful activity and enhances children's verbal skills, creativity, and understanding of narrative structure. For an added layer of engagement, incorporate elements from your immediate surroundings or experiences you've shared, making the stories personal and memorable.

## TALKING ABOUT DREAMS

Discussing dreams can be both a fascinating and calming quiet-time activity. Encourage children to share dreams they've had during sleep or daydreams about their hopes for the future. This opens up a space for them to reflect on their inner thoughts and aspirations, fostering a sense of self-awareness and emotional expression. It can also be a bonding experience, as sharing dreams and aspirations is an incredibly personal activity that can strengthen your connection with the child. Moreover, discussing the content of dreams can lead to interesting conversations about feelings, creativity, and the sometimes bizarre logic of dream sequences, providing insight into the child's mind and helping them to understand their thoughts and feelings better.

Quiet time doesn't have to be a dull or unwelcome part of the day. By incorporating activities that promote relaxation while engaging the mind and heart, we can help children see the value in slowing down and enjoying moments of calm. Whether through the gentle touch of drawing on skin, the imaginative journey of storytelling, or the introspective sharing of dreams, quiet time can be transformed into a cherished opportunity for rest, connection, and reflection. These activities support children's need for physical rest and nurture their emotional well-being and creative spirit, making quiet time something to look forward to.

# CONCLUSION

As we draw the curtains on this journey of joy, creativity, and bonding, I hope that "An Aunt's Guidebook To... Making Memories & Having Fun!" has not only provided you with a treasure trove of activities to enrich your time with the little ones in your life but also inspired you to explore the limitless potential of imagination and play. From the laughter-filled chaos of outdoor adventures to the quiet, introspective moments spent indoors, each chapter was crafted with love and the sincere wish to make your role as an aunt, uncle, parent, grandparent, or guardian as delightful and memorable as possible.

Remember, the heart of this guidebook is not about filling time but creating moments that, when pieced together, form the mosaic of a cherished childhood.

The activities we've explored are merely stepping stones to a deeper connection with the children in your care, a way to teach them about the world and themselves while learning more about your capacity for wonder and joy.

As you continue on this adventure, I encourage you to revisit these pages whenever you need inspiration—or, better yet, let them be a springboard for your creative ideas. The magic of making memories is in the innovation and spontaneity of each shared experience.

Finally, if this guidebook has lit a spark of joy in your journey, please consider leaving a review on Amazon. Your feedback supports my work and helps other caregivers find new ways to enrich their time with the young explorers in their lives. Let's spread the joy of discovery, one shared moment at a time.

Thank you for letting me share in your adventure. Here's to countless memories yet to be made, laughter yet to fill our days, and stories that await in the simple, splendid act of spending time together.

# REFERENCES

OpenAI. (2021). ChatGPT (GPT-4) [Software]. OpenAI. https://www.openai.com/

*Home - Hands on as we Grow®*. (2017, February 16). Hands on as We Grow®. https://handsonaswegrow.com/

Made in the USA
Columbia, SC
23 February 2025

54229116R00033